Jack it UP!

Leverage Your Way to Greater Profits

Best Practices for Networking Success

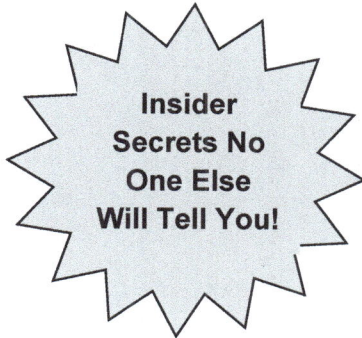

Insider Secrets No One Else Will Tell You!

Turn Talk into Clients

AMBER
Remember to
Jack it Up!
Jack

By Jack Klemeyer

Dedication

Books such as this do not come from one single person. It comes as the culmination of opportunities, experiences and people who have stepped up and offered their hand. For me, that group includes Jim Haskins, who hired me as a greenhorn and taught me how to find success; John Claxon who taught me what it means and takes to be a real leader; Tim Hosey, who initially taught me the thrill and techniques of networking; Tony Scelzo who took my networking to a whole new level; Hazel Walker and Travis Sims for showing me the importance of networking strategy and discipline; Teresa Ray who showed me the power of a network; Cinda Kelley, who gave me opportunity to be myself; Harvey MacKay, who taught me the value of networking personally and through his book, *Swim With the Sharks Without Being Eaten Alive*; Scott Manning who let me see my value through the eyes of others; Dan Kennedy who made me understand the value of a book; Elaine Whitesides and David Yearwood who helped me make it happen; Mom, Dad, Cathy, Melissa, Libby, John and Tommy Richardson for their unwavering love and support; and all the hundreds of professionals I have watched and emulated through the years. Thank you all for touching my heart and mind.

Note about Networking and Growing Your Business

Many so-called professional coaches or consultants may tell you that networking to grow your business is a waste of time; that it doesn't work to grow a business. Well, that's usually because they don't know how to do it correctly, or they have very few, if any, real people skills.

But you can decide for yourself if networking works to grow your business by implementing the strategies and tactics I share with you in this book.

This book gives you exactly what you need to be an expert at getting more of your ideal client at the fee(s) you want; not the clients and fee(s) you've settled for in the past.

To your success!

Jack Klemeyer

Best Practices for Networking Success

Although this book is about strategy and tactics and not about mindset or attitude… the following story illustrates most people's attitude about opportunity and for that matter marketing and networking.

Imagine a guy, we'll call him John. He's in bed at 4:30 in the morning and the phone rings. As he comes out of a sound sleep to answer it, he hears a friend say, 'Hey, I found some gold in my backyard. Come on over and help me dig it up. You can have as much as you can dig up.'

John, eager to roll over and resume his slumber, replies, 'Well, it's early. I don't want to get up this early.'

'No, you don't understand,' his friend says. 'If you dig the gold up, you can have the gold. Whatever you can find, you can have.'

'Well, I don't have a shovel,' John says.

'Get a shovel,' the friend says. 'Go buy one and get over here!' 'Do you know how much they want for shovels these days?'

In the end, John doesn't dig up any gold at all, but he does get some sleep.

Just like the story illustrates, we have many reasons, excuses – mostly BS – of why we do not grow our businesses. But there are reasons underlying all those excuses. Over the course of my experience working with small companies, big companies, and companies in all different industries, I have identified some intrinsic obstacles that impede businesses' growth. Just for giggles, we are going to explore some of them to see if you fall victim to them.

1. **Lack of Focus** – I've got a lot going on, but am not getting things done.
2. **Confidence** – I'm a little scared, I'm not sure how to sell, I'm not sure how to talk to people.
3. **Time Management** – There's never enough day to get everything done, right.
4. **Direction** – I want to go the right way, but I'm not sure which way I should be going with my business.

All of these issues play into the reasons why networking is sometimes not as effective for business owners as it could, or should, be. However, if you look at networking as a way to fill your sales funnel (some call it a pipeline) and consciously create a well-thought out and purposeful process, you can plan your way to networking success. And that networking success can make a real difference in the profitability of your business.

Using Networking Events Effectively

Let me share a simple strategy I learned from my friend Lorraine Ball that I have used successfully. When people attending a networking event enter the room they invariably go to, move, or look to their right. When you have a booth at an event where your prospects will be attending, make sure your booth is to the right of the door. In the same way, if you position yourself to the right of the main entry door, as people enter they will come directly to you.

Get ready with skills and tools

One of the first things effective networkers know that makes them effective is how the Doppler Effect works. You might remember it from science class, but it should also be included in public speaking classes as well. Let me explain with an illustration:

When a train goes by, it's loudest when it's right there in front of you. As it speeds past and gets further away, the horn sound drops off. The volume of the sound doesn't change; it's just that it is no longer right in front of you.

The same is true in a room of people. When you are facing a group and speaking in their direction, they can hear and understand you. When you have your back to the audience or cannot be seen, your message can easily be lost, or worse, misinterpreted.

What you need to know is this:

If you are asked to introduce yourself,

1. Stand up and position yourself so you are facing the majority of the audience.
2. Do not begin speaking until you are fully standing.
3. Speak clearly, loudly and slowly.
4. Do not begin to sit down until you are completely done talking.

Now those are just the mechanics. Just as much consideration has to go into what you say. Who will remember you and your business when they need you if you simply say, "I'm a bookkeeper," and sit down?

Your moment in the spotlight should include three critical elements:

1. Your name and the name of your business
2. The hook and meat about your business
3. Contact information or an invitation

Giving your name and the name of your business is easy – or at least it should be. If it's not, call me and we'll work through that. Really, sometimes that is not clear for new business owners and I'm happy to help bring clarity on that.

The meat about your business is a short statement that gets to the heart of what products or services you provide in your business. And the hook is that little pointy edge that helps them to remember you. For instance, I have a friend who has a water extraction business. You know, when your basement floods or you have a fire and there is water damage from the fire department putting out a fire. Their hook – their tagline – was "Everybody sucks, but we suck better." You'll remember that, won't you? My tagline is "If your business isn't growing, you don't know Jack!" Now these may be a little irreverent, but I know they are memorable because the proof comes in the frequency of when people point at me and say with a big grin, "I remember you – I don't know Jack!"

The final point, providing an invitation or contact information can come in many different forms. Some people give out their telephone number or website URL. Others invite the audience to an upcoming event or offer a cup of coffee and conversation. It depends on what you have scheduled and what you feel best fits your business at that time – what you are trying to achieve.

So, you're at the event, you stand up and the spotlight shines and your talk goes great. After the program, you find yourself surrounded by people who want to get to know you. Are you ready? You will be if you remembered to bring a couple of things. These are not just suggestions. ALWAYS have them with you when you are networking – or going through your regular day. You never know when you will meet the next most important client or colleague!

You will look professional, organized and ready to service clients if you do. And you know how important that first impression is to future business. So, listen up. Maybe I should put this list in capitals....

1. YOUR BUSINESS CARDS
2. PEN OR PENCIL AND PAPER

Now that's not so difficult, is it? No, it's not. But if you don't have those things, you have no way to give a prospect a way to get hold of you or for you to get in contact with them. And isn't that the whole purpose of networking? You might just as well not even attend if you are going to be there without the tools you need.

Just do it, okay? Here are some tips to help you have business cards ready every day.

Your business cards

First, think about your own cards. They will probably be that one and only thing that the people you meet will have when the networking event is over. Not only that, it will probably be one in a whole pile of cards collected on that day, in that week or even month.

So you need to ensure that it does three things:

1. It accurately reflects who you are and the services that you or your business provides
2. It provides all the necessary information so you can be contacted after networking events
3. You will be remembered

So here are my top tips for brilliant business cards:

1. When choosing a card ensure that you know what message you want to convey and that the card reflects both what you do and 'who you are' from an image point of view. Use the services of a professional graphic designer who will design something that eye-catching but appropriate to what you represent.
2. Ensure the quality of your card reflects the quality of your products or services.
3. Avoid dark backgrounds which prevent contacts from making valuable notes on them.
4. Include essential details on your card so you can be contacted:· Your name· Company name· The telephone number of where you like to be contacted· E-mail address· Postal address.

5. Include key words and phrases which sum up what you do - even better how your products or services can help.

6. Use a catchy tagline to help convey an overall message about what you do.

7. Consider using the AIDA sequence (Attention, Interest, Desire, Action) to help lay out your card.

8. Make your card interactive e.g. I put the 'wheel of life' on the back of my coaching cards and sometimes get people to complete it on the spot. It creates interest and helps explain an aspect of how I help people.

9. One of the best tools to help people remember you is to put a photo on your card.

10. Use both sides of the card as this maxes out on the space available

11. If you have a limited budget, consider buying from the ranges of free and low cost cards available on the Internet eg. Vista print and Goodprint.

12. Consider buying a card case – these keep your cards in good condition and provide a useful place to put the ones you have received.

13. Always keep a good supply of cards with you so you always have them to hand wherever you go, networking events or otherwise.

Figure out why you are networking

It is important to understand that there is a system at play or there certainly should be one in place behind your networking. As a matter of fact, it should be behind all of your marketing efforts. My friend, fellow coach and author of the must-have book, *Get Clients Now!*™, C.J. Hayden, demonstrates that system as the Universal Marketing Cycle™. It is one of the best illustrated examples of the system of a person serious about growing their business should follow.

Universal Marketing Cycle

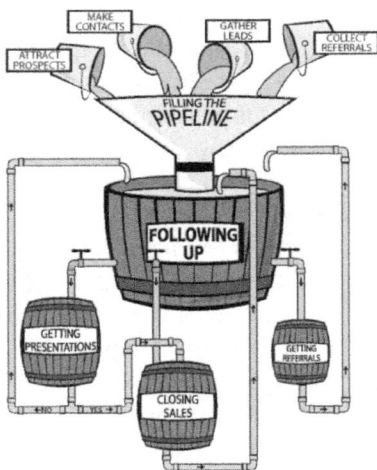

You can see that there are four main parts to the cycle:

1. Filling the Pipeline
2. Following Up
3. Getting Presentations
4. Closing the Sale

And, in addition to these four above and illustrated, I like to add one more, it is shown on the system, and that's Collecting Referrals.

Your prospects and clients should be moving through this cycle at the various stages all the time. However, when the system is not in place or there is a clog in the pipeline, then the whole cycle begins to slow and eventually stops completely. Unfortunately, for some who do not have a system like this in place, they do not have to wait for it to shut down because it already is shut down. Understanding the Universal Marketing Cycle and recognizing where your weakness is or where you're struggling right now is the key to your success.

Now that you have the tools and skills all set up, let's talk about the reason to go through all this rigmarole. (Love that word, don't you?)

You need to have a clearly defined outcome. Ask:

- Why are you going to the meeting?
- What do you want to give at the meeting?
- What do you want to get from the meeting?

Don't walk in until you have a clear goal in mind. You might want to meet someone in particular you expect to be there. If so, you walk in ready to ask if someone knows the person and if they would introduce you.

If your goal is to make contacts for prospective clients or referral sources, you MUST know who your target market is and who you are looking to connect with at the event. Remember, it may be a social, casual event, but if you are looking at it as a networking opportunity, treat it seriously and focus on it like you would other business tasks.

It's important to know who your ideal target audience is when you are networking and this illustration shows you why that is true. This little graphic, once understood and applied to your business strategy, will liberate you and provide you with immense leverage and freedom.

Marketing
Ideal Client
Preferred
Your Speciality

Can Do!
Tolerated Client
Capible of Doing

Sales
Second Best Client
Can Do

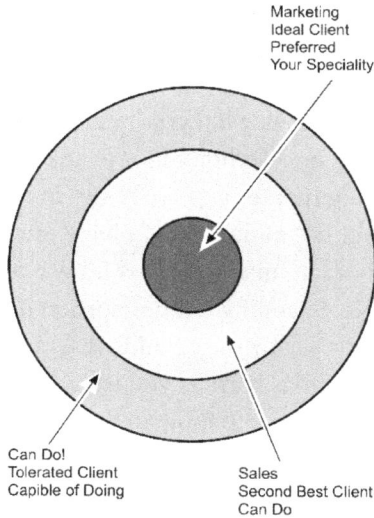

The center of the bulls-eye represents the clients, products and services you specialize in. It's your Ideal Target Market, prospect or client. These are the people you enjoy working with the most, your profit is at its best with this group and you know how they think and feel. You know their wants, needs and desires. When you zero in on this group you have your best success.

The next ring, the second ring out, is the people who want the things you can do and you are more or less willing to do. You reach this market by selling to it or fulfilling a need your ideal client has or requests. This could be ancillary services to your ideal client or selling to your second best client type.

The outside ring is what you're capable of providing, doing or offering, but it is not working with the market you are really excited about servicing. It's almost like "I have to... to make money!" That, my friends, is no way to have a business. Spending a large portion of your time on this sector only builds resentment and problems. And as hard as you try, you will always have dissatisfied people in this ring. It is almost as if the harder you try to accommodate them, the more they expect or demand from you. That builds the resentment.

This bulls-eye model provides a clear illustration of how to focus your marketing and selling efforts. Here's a hint, it is much easier and much more profitable to move from the inside, the ideal, to the outer rings. You can make that migration by choice rather than by force of necessity. When you, as most do, try to move from the outer ring to the inner target it is much more difficult.

Navigating any business endeavor, especially marketing and selling from the point of necessity is a much more difficult journey. When that happens, the mindset a person possesses is usually coming from a position of resentment because you are dealing with the clients you are capable of serving but who are not preferred or even desired. Here's why... since you are not coming from your preferred or desired area you do not have the resources or the resources are tight. When your resources, energy, focus, comfort and money are scarce, you do not perform nearly as well as if you had all those things present or in abundance.

Figure out how to harvest new clients

One of the most satisfying moments in coaching new small business owners and entrepreneurs is when they realize that there are new clients out there everywhere, if they know how to look for them. Here are three sure fire strategies for you.

Strategy One: many have never heard of is the Food Chain. The Food Chain is simply providing goods or services to another business or customer. For example, someone who sells water conditioners would have a potential customer in new home owners or even home builders. So find new subdivisions or builders and connect with the builders and homeowners. You become part of the Food Chain. You feed

your business off other businesses who have
your customers or who set up the situation for
new customers. Does that make sense?

Strategy Two: Another way to harvest new
clients is to identify a Niche in the marketplace
that you service. Going back to the home builder
example, if you are a copper worker like another
friend of mine, you would identify top of the
line builders in an area with big or nice houses
to market your services to the owners. They
would be interested in custom copper sinks,
range hoods or counter tops for their custom
kitchens.

Once you have identified the market, you
have to do two things.

1. You have to determine where the
    people you want to connect with
    hang out. Where can you find them?
    And then you have to put yourself in
    those places.
2. You have to answer the question,
    "Who is the decision maker?" For
    the copper worker, the decision
    maker could be the owner of a
    home-building company or the
    design executive. For a homeowner,
    it might be the husband or the wife.

Then, and you know what I'm going to say, you have to get yourself around those people. And networking events might be the way to do that.

Strategy Three: Watch for a "Trigger Event." A trigger event could be a house being built or it could be a mortgage foreclosure. Sometimes decisions have already been made by the time you see the new construction or for sale sign, but not always. Another may be an announcement that a builder will be starting a new subdivision in your area or that a new plant is coming to town, which might attract new building and new residents – and feed right into the client base you want to build.

Now that you know these strategies, you might have a new perspective on where to find potential clients. But here's the secret:

People do business with people they know, like and trust.

That comes down to relationships and you've got to be in a place to meet people so they can get to know you or something about you. You know where that leads you, don't you? Yes, back to networking and community involvement.

To continue on with this line of thinking, when you meet people, you've got to be likeable. Likeability is a huge factor in the influence a person has on another. So even if you have had a challenging day that has left you tired and crabby, make an effort to take off the cranky face and sporting a smile, thinking and saying positive things. It will go a long way to present the likeable person inside you, which is the one you want everyone to know and remember.

The last element is trust. Usually the pattern goes that people get to know you, they get to like you or see something in you that is like them, some similarity, then over time, if you do what you say you're going to do and follow through with promises, trust develops. It's how a relationship is formed and that is how you do business – it is relationships.

Building Relationships

A strategy critical to successful networking is relationship building. Generating business through referrals or 'positive recommendations' comes when people have come to know, like and trust you. To make that happen takes concerted time and effort on your part – and a conscious strategy, too. In order to help you in your journey, here are the top tips that I have gathered over the years for building successful business relationships:

KNOW

1. Be able to succinctly describe the benefits of your service.
2. If you can't describe them, how can others?
3. Be specific about the help you want – who do you want referrals to?
4. How can someone recognize that someone else needs your service?
5. How effective are your business cards – do they clearly convey what you do? Do you use both sides?
6. Do you have effective promotional material that clearly conveys how you/your services are of value to others?

LIKE

1. Help others first.
2. Never criticize others.
3. Provide written and verbal testimonials whenever possible. In fact, other them.
4. Be supportive to others when they need it.

TRUST

1. Be authentic – don't try to be someone you are not – remember it is 'you' that is your unique selling point and people will see through an 'act'.
2. Deliver your promises and exceed expectations with the service you provide.
3. Be a good customer – pay on time.

If you are going from networking event to networking event and not getting any business from it, and you're making calls day after day, it's time to stop, step back and reassess. Ask yourself some important questions:

- Am I likeable?
- Are people getting to know me?
- Am I getting to know them?
- What am I missing?

There is a gap somewhere and you've got to figure out where that is and you do that by answering – honestly – those questions. Look over time, not just at one event, what's happened? What's NOT happened? Time is a great illuminator and looking for and identifying significant patters will be most helpful in the long run.

We all have a learning curve and in order to shorten your curve, I want to give you some of the tips, strategies and important bits of information I have gathered to improve my own networking through the years.

Rapport

Building rapport is one of the fundamental business networking skills to master so here are 10 networking tips for success and how to avoid being a rapport wrecker.

Remember networking is all about building relationships with people…NOT about selling and the first step in any relationship building is to establish a level of rapport with the other person so you are having a genuine conversation rather than stilted small talk which party is interested in.

Once someone feels connected with you they will naturally want to find out more about what you do, help you and possibly in the longer term buy from you or refer your services.

So, how do you build rapport?

1. Make eye contact and smile.

2. Introduce yourself using your first name only.

3. Repeat their name – it always makes people feel good hearing their name *and* it helps you to remember it.

4. Start off by asking really easy small talk questions like 'have you been to these events before?, 'who do you know here?' and of course, 'what do you do?'

5. Look for 'things in common' to talk about – perhaps there are people you know in common, or are based in the same town or your businesses are related.

6. Ask further questions related to what the other person has said which shows you are listening and that you are interested.

7. Listen…and show that you are listening.

8. Build on what they have said e.g. 'the food is good here' …'yes, it is, I particularly like… .'

9. Ask for their business card and make related comments 'Ah yes, I have heard of your company before – how long have you been established?'

10. Keep your comments positive at all times.
11. 'Mirror' their body language. This is one of the most interesting business networking skills - research has shown that people who are in rapport with each other display matching or mirror image body language. Similarly you can build rapport by copying their body language – don't worry they won't notice! This is just one of many NLP (Neuro Linguistic Programming) techniques.

Now you can master business networking, just take on board the networking tips to avoid becoming a rapport wrecker.

Rapport Wreckers

Building rapport can take a few minutes or more, destroying it can take seconds. So what are some of the biggest rapport wreckers that should be avoided at all costs?

1. Disagreeing with the person you have just met however trivial the point may be – (an exception to this is if someone

makes an offensive remark which you would not want to be party to in which case you would not want to build rapport anyway).

2. Talking too much – remember you are trying to develop a two way conversation, not give a speech.
3. Giving a sales pitch.
4. Criticizing others.
5. Halitosis (You know, bad breath...)
6. Always having to be "right."
7. Any negative comments.
8. Always looking away from the person you are talking to, at your watch, your phone, people coming in the room, etc.

Not everyone is good at small talk and initiating conversations. If that tends to describe you, here are 10 Feel-Good Questions from my friend, author and speaker, Bob Burg to get you started at your next networking event:

1. How did you get your start in the 'widget' business?
2. What do you enjoy most about what you do?
3. What separates your company from your competition?

4. What advice would you give someone just starting in the widget (his or her) business?
5. What one thing would you do with your business if you knew you couldn't fail?
6. What significant changes have you seen take place in your profession through the years?
7. What do you see as the coming trends in the widget business?
8. Describe the strangest (or funniest) incident you've ever experienced in your business?
9. What ways have you found to be the most effective for promoting your business?
10. What one sentence would you like people to use in describing the way you do business?

Those are great questions to get to know others, but if you want the magic question that will start to build rapport and that relationship, be sure to remember Bob Burg's One "Key" Question That Will Set You Apart From Everyone Else ...

How can I know if someone I'm talking to would be a good prospect for you?

Referability

Imagine how great it would be to have your clients saying about you, "This is the person you are looking for. Call her today!"

Or, if you are in the corporate environment, to have your team members or colleagues suggesting you for the next great job promotion.

The goal is to have plenty of business through referrals and to have business from referrals be a major contributor to your bottom line.

Here's a great piece of advice from strategic coach Dan Sullivan on the Law of Referability.

The Law of Referability by **Dan Sullivan:**

"The best way to grow any business is by word of mouth. Here are the four habits that will make people want to refer you.

Every success you've achieved or will achieve in the future is tied to a relationship. So one of the most powerful abilities an entrepreneur can develop is *referability* – being someone whom your best customers want to introduce to other people like them.

Many people strive to be in this position, but what they've never stopped to consider exactly what makes other people want to give a good referral. For example, lots of people in this world are intelligent, good looking, and have a great sense of humor, but things still aren't going their way. They have all sorts of wonderful qualities, but people wouldn't consider referring them to anyone whose opinion they care about.

Why? I believe it's because they've failed to establish and reinforce four crucial habits. I call these The Referability Habits™. In order to be referred, anywhere in the world, under any circumstances, you have to have these four habits as the basis of your performance:

1. **Show up on time.**
2. **Do what you say.**
3. **Finish what you start.**
4. **Say please and thank you.**

These seem like common sense, don't they? You may be thinking, "This is kids' stuff. Surely there must be more to being referred than this." Look closer.

Each of these four habits is based on showing respect and appreciation for other people. Every person you meet is the center of his or her own universe; when you demonstrate from the very beginning of a relationship through your habitual behavior that you recognize the central importance of the other person's schedule, commitments, deadlines, and goals, you immediately become an invaluable resource in their life. He or she will want to refer you into other important situations and relationships.

By focusing on relationship, you multiply opportunities for yourself and your business. The secret is to provide extraordinary service to an inner circle of high quality clients and centers of influence. They, in turn, become marketers for you through referrals to other individuals like them. By doing this in a systematic fashion, you're able to create an unlimited high quality market that's immune to the ups and downs of local and national economies.

Keep in mind that these habits must be an integral part of your daily life. They aren't tactics you can adopt for a short duration or just until a deal is closed. There are all sorts of other strategies for being successful, but if those strategies don't include these four habits, they will never work. Mastering The Referability Habits create your future."

Reap the benefits of the networking event

So the event went well and you are going home with a pocketful of business cards. Woohoo! You get home and what happens to those cards? If you are like many small business owners, they end up one of several places:

1. In a desk drawer
2. In a "special box or basket"
3. In a stack on the desk
4. In the trash

None of those common places does you any good, do they? Why spend all the time and effort to network if that is what is going to happen the next day? It's not true that all you have to do is wait for them to call you...you might get a call once in a while, but sporadic calls are not going to be the basis of a thriving business.

What you need is a process, a system, for following up, touching base and eventually turning the name on the business card into a client; a simple, step-by-step follow-up system to use after you attend networking events.

When you attend those networking events like a chamber of commerce meeting, trade show or small business fair and you end up with a stack of business cards, there is a strategy to implement to ensure the best results. And you will find with each use it becomes simpler and simpler – because it just makes sense!

Take the business cards you've collected at the networking event, spread them out on your desk or a table and then divide them into three piles; A, B, and C.

Pile A – Prospective Clients: comprised of those cards who are prospective clients, those who people or companies who could be your client.

Pile B – Useful Networking Contacts: comprised of those cards that are useful networking contacts. These are people or contacts that may be able to help you get business.

Pile C - People who are neither prospective clients nor useful networking contacts. Unless you want a personal relationship with these people, they are not worth following up on, and don't belong in your contact management system. A word of warning though… be careful who you judge to not be useful to you.

Next, sort Pile A into three stacks: **Hot Leads** - those you might have had a conversation with at the networking event; **Warm Leads** - those you can or plan to get an introduction to very soon; and **Cool Leads** - those that you can build a strategy to get to meet or follow-up within the very near future. You will want to follow up immediately with both the hot and warm leads.

Now sort your Pile B, "useful networking contacts" into two stacks. **Stack One** includes those you want to follow-up now, cards of people that can lead to clients and those with people who may have leads or referrals for you. **Stack Two** are the cards of those people who could be marketing opportunities.

Here are three-step follow-up processes for each group of cards:

With Pile A - Hot Leads: This is someone who has already expressed an interest in doing business with you. Step 1: Call each, reintroduce yourself, and try to make your pitch or get an appointment to do so. Step 2: When you get voicemail, send a letter or email. Step 3: Put them on your follow-up calendar.

With Pile A - Warm Leads: This is

someone who mentioned a problem or goal you know you can help with in their business. Step 1: Call each, reintroduce yourself, and try to make your pitch or get an appointment to do so. Step 2: When you get voicemail, send a letter or email. Step 3: Add them to a follow-up calendar.

With Pile B - Useful Networking Contacts (Stack One): These are the people you believe can lead you directly to prospective clients. Step 1: Call each. Suggest coffee, lunch or offer to stop by their office. Step 2: Work to build an ongoing relationship. Listen for clues about their interests, concerns and goals. Step 3: Consider what or how you may be able to offer to create reciprocity in our relationship.

There are three piles left: Cool leads from Pile A, Marketing Opportunities from Pile B and Other which is all of Pile C.

The Cool Leads from Pile A: These are people in your target market whose needs you know nothing about. Step 1: Send a nice-to-meet-you note; handwritten makes a much bigger impact. Step 2: Put these people in your contact management system in case you need them later. Step 3: Put them in your relationship building process.

Marketing Opportunities (Stack Two) from Pile B: These are people who can lead you to other marketing opportunities. If you are looking for new marketing opportunities as part of you current plan, contact these people. Otherwise treat them as "Cool Leads" from Pile A above.

This leaves us with all of the cards in Pile C. These are people who are neither prospective clients nor useful networking contacts. Again, unless you want a personal relationship with these people, they are not worth following up, and don't belong in your contact management system. Remember too the caveat to be very careful who you judge to not be useful to you. I personally put these folks on my weekly email list to keep in touch. You never know who they know or how they might refer you.

This process may seem hard, but it is really not. It is just complicated, so if you'd like an infographic about this whole process, go to my website at GYBCoaching.com (use this link: http://bit.ly/1crxVsn) where you can download it. The visual explanation illustrates this process for a clearer understanding and help in implementation.

About being referred…

If you are like me you might be concerned about how you are introduced to a prospective client or referral partner. I know I was until my good friend and client, Matt Maudlin of Memo Marketing (http://memomarketinggroup.com) and I created *Tell'em'boutMe!*

Tell'em'boutMe! is a very simple tool that allows you to control how you are introduced and referred. Just as important is the fact that the person who introduced you gets a thank-you email, the person they introduced you to gets an introduction email and you get an email telling you who you were introduced to and how you might be a fit. All this can be tracked as a subscriber through your unique login to the dashboard toolbox in the *Tell'em'boutMe!* system. If I sound excited about this tool... I am, because it works! Take a look at http://tellemboutme.com. One of my clients received 104 referrals in a 10-day period!

Follow-up after speed networking events

Sometimes you will attend an event like a speed networking event where you have the opportunity to say specifically the target market you wish to meet. People with contacts that fit your market share their cards with you. You share your card when you have contacts to share with them. Your next step is to follow-up with them to pursue those leads and to see how you can help them pursue their target.

There are three possible options to follow-up:

1. Send an email to people who gave you cards saying they might have a contact:

For example:

Hi (name on card),

Thank you for giving me your card at (name the event).

Let me remind you what I do (tell about your business) and who I am looking to meet (target market).

I appreciate any assistance you can provide, and let me know how I might be able to help you.

Your name

Your contact information

2. Make a call to people if they had a particular contact in mind.

For example:

Hi (name on card), this is (your name) and we met at the (name of event). You gave me your business card when I mentioned I wanted to meet (your target market), and I am following up with you to see if you wouldn't mind to make an introduction for me?

3. Making an introduction

You raised your card and offered to make an introduction for someone else. It is your responsibility to follow up with the introduction. You are emailing that person you had in mind when you raised your card to inform them you have a new contact and want to introduce them.

For example:

Hi (person you know),

I hope you are enjoying this nice Thursday afternoon. I want to introduce you to (person from networking event). (He/She) is a (describe what they do) and is looking to meet (example: realtors on the North side of Indianapolis), so immediately I thought of you. I encourage you to reach out to (name) and see how you can help one another. (Give networking contact information here, and possible CC them to email.)

Thanks and have a great day.

Your name
Your contact information

At the Very Least

As you are starting to develop your process, don't miss out on business because your process isn't completely set up. Use this very simple follow-up process to get you moving:

Step 1. Meet Prospect A at an event, enter his name and contact information into database.

Step 2. Send prospect an email greeting. Remind him where you met and what you do. Say it was a pleasure to meet and you hope to see him again.

Step 3. Call or send an email suggest a face-to-face meeting over a cup of coffee to learn more about each other and how you can work together and promote each other.

Step 4. Meet.

Step 5. Send a promotional advertising piece in the mail.

It's an established, automatic way to handle every prospect you meet. You can use an app or software to make correspondence go out automatically and you only have to respond to emails or calls the recipient sends to you.

Want to really knock the socks off a prospect? Send them a handwritten note. It doesn't have to be fancy or long. It can just be a card saying, "Nice to meet you last night. See you soon!" Boom. Done. Drop it in the mail.

You know what? It is just as easy to not do these things as it is to do them. And your business will grow if you make the choice to make it happen. If you want your sales to grow, if you want to do better, get a system. It's that simple. Set up a system.

Is email the answer?

How many times have you, when following up with a prospect, sent them an email? If that is the only way you are following up with prospects and current clients, then I have news for you: You are not following up!

One of the biggest pet peeves I have when working with clients who want more sales, need more sales and sometimes are desperate for sales tell me, "I sent them an email," when I have asked if they have followed up with their prospects.

The real way, the best way and as far as I am concerned, the only true way to follow up is to pick up your phone and call them or drop by and check in on them. Anything else and you are only fooling yourself and probably losing more sales than you realize.

At a recent event in Chicago, I heard Dan Kennedy talk about online and off line marketing and the results or lack of results with each. Dan said that "even customers who tell you they want only digital (that means email) correspondence, follow-up, etc. are in fact, not satisfied with the only digital approach. He cited an investment firm that was averaging a 34 percent annual renewal rate on one of their subscription programs with printed renewal notices. After "listening" to their clients who requested to go to digital only correspondence, their annual renewal rate dropped to a meager 12 percent in only two years.

Let's look at real dollars for the same scenario. That investment firm was making $720 per client annually when they used a print renewal form, but when they switched to the digital, i.e. email, the average annual income per person dropped to only (meager again) $190 per client. This after 70 percent of the firm's client's were "eager for digital only."

The tragedy is that many who say "I sent them and email" believe that it is an effective way to follow-up, correspond or communicate. Albeit only one example, the example is strong enough to encourage us all to at least do a test, or worst case, pay attention to our results.

Next time, pick up the phone or send them something in the mail. Do not, in any case, just rely on email to be your follow-up mechanism.

It's all a system

Yes, this networking strategy is indeed just a system, isn't it? I mean think about it. There are steps you have to take, things you have to decide and do, and stay on track – one foot after another. Let's review:

- You have to meet people and fill your sales pipeline or funnel.

- You have to identify your market.
- You have to set a goal for each event.
- You have to identify where you will meet those people.
- You have to present a professional and polished message and behavior.
- You have to build relationships.
- You have to have a system to follow-up on new contacts.

That's a whole lot of "have-to" items on a list, isn't it? But the important thing to remember is that once you set up a regular systematic way to handle the whole picture, the feeling of such a long list will go away. You won't have to think about the steps and plan each one because it will become second nature. It's just the way it should be handled.

And the reason is simple – you want to meet people, get to know them and stay in touch so when they need a service or product you can provide, THEY CALL *YOU*.

Is your business ready?

It is a great feeling when the phone rings and emails pop into your inbox with requests for your services. Networking the right way can do that for you. But you want to be certain that you are ready to handle the growth in a stable, healthy way. And sometimes we don't know the real status of our business. I can help with that.

Take a FREE assessment for a "snap shot" of the heath of your business at http://mybusinesscheckup.com .

I promise it will give you an idea of where you stand ... and where you need help.

Back to the obstacles

One of the greatest obstacles I see when I work with new (or long-time) business owners is that they feel there is just too much – too much to do; too much to organize, plan, implement or try. What we do is work through everything one step at a time. Just like putting together the system to make networking work for you. Start at the beginning and work through it. The same is true for every one of these obstacles.

4. **Lack of Focus** – I've got a lot going on and not getting things done
5. **Confidence** – I'm a little scared, I'm not sure how to sell, I'm not sure how to talk to people

6. **Time Management** – There's never enough day to get everything done, right
7. **Direction** – I'm not sure which way I should be going with my business

You probably know which ones are your biggest stumbling blocks. So, for the time being, forget the others and take one step to give yourself some relief in that one area. For instance,

If **Lack of Focus** has your name written all over it, consider time blocking. Set one hour to work on one thing, without distraction. See how much you get done. You don't have to change your entire schedule, just try it for one or two hours a day. If it works, increase the time blocks. Adjust it to meet the needs of your business.

If **Confidence** is where you feel least, well, confident, start small. Don't necessarily set out to sell to everyone you meet. Just make a point to talk to two new people every day. Or set a goal of five new contacts at a networking event. Keep building on it. It doesn't have to be perfect, be yourself, make friends and build relationships.

If **Time Management** keeps you at your desk or on the phone long after others have gone home for the day, ask yourself if you are expending too much effort on tasks or projects that are either not making money or are not really important. Maybe it doesn't really matter if the notes from every meeting are transcribed and entered into your project management program. Or that every photo from an event is resized for social media use. Only include the information, notes or photos required and see how much time you save. Give important and money-making tasks priority, then let go of the rest.

If **Direction** leaves you stymied, the best solution I have is to get help. Whether you opt to work one-on-one with a coach or become a member of a group coaching meeting or a Mastermind, having someone else to bounce ideas and talk with can help you clarify your thinking, your purpose and what you want your business – and life – to become over the short- or long-term.

Remember, business owners don't build successful businesses alone. There are a lot of people teaching, guiding, supporting, encouraging and simply standing beside them as they grow. You can find the support and learning you need – and give the support and benefit of your experience to others.

If you don't think it's any of these four, but you've been struggling to get things going in your business it could be a condition where you hesitate to prospect for new clients on a consistent daily basis. This condition is responsible for the failure of more competent, motivated, capable salespeople than any other single factor. As a matter of fact nothing else even comes close and we need to talk sooner than later. I offer a complementary consultation to help people identify their specific situation and then help with a strategy to overcome this condition. Simply go to my website click the link and complete the Complementary Consultation form. Fix it now!

Start networking to grow your business. Set a goal, implement these ideas and you'll be amazed where it takes you!

Final Thoughts

Share this book and others in the Jack it UP! Series to help others *Leverage Their Way to Greater Profits.* Special offer available for bulk purchases. For more information, contact Hannah@GYBCoaching.com.

Share your successes. Send us your thoughts, insights, wins and success stories. We would love to hear how these things helped so we can use those with future projects and in new projects. Mail or email to:

> Great Success
> c/o Grow Your Business Coaching
> P.O. Box 496
> Brownsburg, IN 46112
> Hannah@GYBCoaching.com

Visit us at GYBCoaching.com for additional insights, hot new information, products and resources.

Thank you to my family, friends and colleagues for the support and encouragement in turning belief, caring and knowledge into action that creates the results for greater profits and success for all.

Grow Your Business™ Coaching Resources for YOUR Business

Networking Follow-Up Process Infographic

Get it FREE at http://bit.ly/1crxVsn and get the system working for you.

Tell'em'boutMe!

Establish your own referral machine with every email you send out. Make the referral message about you and your business exactly what you want it to be with simple, easy to use, *Tell'em'boutMe!* Go to Tellemboutme.com.

Small Business Check-up

Take a FREE assessment to get a "snap shot" of the health of your business. Figure out where the gaps are that hold you back. Go to http://mybusinesscheckup.com

Complementary Consultation

A Complementary 45-minute Consultation with Jack Klemeyer will help to identify and prioritize challenges you face with your business and whether a coach like Jack can help you move forward. This 45-minute conversation could be the start of the change your business needs. Schedule it today at GYBCoaching.com.

Special Resources

Whitesides Words encourages all professionals to share their experience and knowledge through the written word including books, articles, ebooks and the like. Owner Elaine Whitesides believes that every person and business has a story to share. She simply provides the assistance and guidance to turn that story and wisdom into a printed product such as this book. Contact her at Elaine@WhitesidesWords.com.

About the Author

Jack Klemeyer, is the founder of Grow Your Business™ Coaching, a coaching company that facilitates high-impact, result-focused group and individual coaching for entrepreneurs and business owners to help them grow their business.

Drawing from his more than 30 years of experience and expertise in effective sales and communication skills, Klemeyer has personally designed and presented several successful programs to aid participants in enhancing their performance.

In addition to being a professional speaker, copywriter, trainer and consultant, he is an accredited facilitator and consultant for a wide variety of programs, including Get Clients Now!™, DiSC, Myers Briggs, and the Kolbe System™. He is also a certified Master Practitioner of Neuro-Linguistic Programming and a certified Language and Behavior Consultant. For more information, go to www.GYBCoaching.com.

QUICK CONTACT FORM

Do you think Jack would bring inspiration, knowledge, skills, mirth and merriment to your organization, next group meeting or training? The only way to find out is to get in touch! And that's easy!

Fax: 317-203-0804
Telephone: 317- 755- 6963
Email: Hannah@GYBCoaching.com
Postal: P. O. Box 496, Brownsburg, IN 46112

Please send more FREE information on:

- ☐ Other books
- ☐ Audio Programs
- ☐ Online Programs
- ☐ Speaking
- ☐ Seminars and Workshops
- ☐ Consulting
- ☐ Individual and Group Coaching

Name: _____

Address: _____

City: _____

State: _____ Zip: _____

Email: _____

QUICK CONTACT FORM

Do you think Jack would bring inspiration, knowledge, skills, mirth and merriment to your next group meeting or training? The only way to find out is to get in touch! And that's easy!

Fax: 317-203-0804
Telephone: 317- 755- 6963
Email: Hannah@GYBCoaching.com
Postal: P. O. Box 496, Brownsburg, IN 46112

Please send more FREE information on:

- ❑ Other books
- ❑ Audio Programs
- ❑ Online Programs
- ❑ Speaking
- ❑ Seminars and Workshops
- ❑ Consulting
- ❑ Individual and Group Coaching

Name: _____

Address: _____

City: _____

State: _____ Zip: _____

Email: _____

Want A Surge of Business Growth Each & Every Month?

Get Your Own Grow Your Business™ Resources Every Month!

You'll get $610.94 of Income-Increasing Information for Only $39.97 With the

Grow Your Business™ INSIGHT Membership

($39.97/Month)

Fax the form on the next page to 317-203-0804

A Surge of Business Growth!

Get Your Own Grow Your Business Resources Every Month!

{You'll get $610.94 of Income Increasing Information for Only $39.97 }

With the Grow Your Business INSIGHT Membership ($39.97/Month): *each month you'll receive...*

- ✓ The monthly **INSIGHT Business Builder Newsletter** chock full of marketing strategies, interviews, Mental Mindset Strategies and business growth concepts. Each issue is it's own mini-seminar delivered to your door giving you a constant stream of "What's Working Now" for entrepreneurs.
- ✓ You'll collect our **Weekly INSIGHT eTips** dedicated to providing inspiration, motivation and resources all geared to increasing your business profits and personal income.
- ✓ You'll receive the monthly Grow Your Business Audio Program, **Real Business Radio**. The program is packed with audio interviews, advanced marketing advice and strategies along with real life examples from successful entrepreneurs, small business owners, business leaders and featured fellow INSIGHT members.
- ✓ **Monthly Group Calls** providing "laser style coaching," information sharing and interviews of member success stories. Each dynamic call is archived for your handy reference any time you need it for a refresher or kick in the butt to get going. *(Available at an additional cost with INSIGHT Plus Membership)*

As a reward for taking action you also get these great bonuses!

BONUS #1: The Complete Goal Getting Seminar in a box ($399.97 Value):

- ✓ This 2 Audio CD set & Guide that outline the critical components necessary to set and achieve your goals, covering both the business and the mental side of Goal Getting, the program presents everything you need to set your goals now and achieve them.

BONUS #2: INSIGHT Deluxe 3-Ring Binder ($27 Value)

- ✓ This Deluxe 3-Ring Binder comes complete with hand picked and trusted resources that you'll have VIP access to as a member of the Grow Your Business program. You'll use it to store each of your monthly editions of the INSIGHT Newsletter.

Month 2 - BONUS: Using Public Relations for Marketing: ($97 Value)

- ✓ Online access to one of Grow Your Business most powerful & impactful presentations. This highly praised online workshop is sure to make you rethink how you can use PR in your business as the centerpiece marketing tool it really is.

Month 3 - BONUS: Using LinkedIn for Profit Audio Program ($47 Value)

- ✓ Complete Audio Program to guide you through the client getting, moneymaking strategies of using LinkedIn.

Yes! I want to trigger a SURGE of Business Growth by taking advantage of everything Grow Your Business INSIGHT has to offer for a full 60 days, plus the additional bonuses for just $39.97!

Name_____ Company_____

Phone_____ Email_____

Credit Card: ____ Visa ____ MasterCard ____ American Express ____ Discover

Credit Card # _____ Exp. _____ Sec. Code _____

Name on Card _____

Billing Street _____ City _____ State ____ Zip_____

SIGNATURE:_____ DATE:_____

What you get as a member!

EACH and EVERY Month YOU Get!

Monthly INSIGHT Newsletter
Jam packed with resources, how-to's, mental game strategies, interviews, insights and much more!

Monthly Audio Program
Interviews with superachievers, how-to's, resources, and much more!

Monthly Group Calls
Calls to keep you up to date, accountable and moving forward with your goals, learn important concepts and share successes.

With Your Membership YOU Get THESE BONUSES!

Deluxe 3-Ring Binder
To hold your issues of INSIGHT for easy reference plus Handpicked Resources for your business already inside when you receive your Membership Package!

Goal Getting Seminar in-a-box
Complete 3 hour plus program packed with strategies goal getters use to reach their goals. Worksheets and complete transcript are included as a BONUS!

Secrets of Using P.R. as Marketing
On demand webinar packed with successful strategies to use Public Relations as a Marketing Tool in your business!

Made in the USA
Middletown, DE
25 March 2019